ON THE WATERFRONT: THE HOTWELLS STORY

ON THE WATERFRONT

THE HOTWELLS STORY

HELEN REID & SUE STOPS

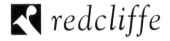

First published in 2002 by Redcliffe Press Ltd.,
81g Pembroke Road, Bristol BS8 3EA

© Helen Reid and Sue Stops

ISBN 1 900178 88 5

British Library Cataloguing in Publication Data
A catalogue record for this book is available from
The British Library

Typeset by Mayhew Typesetting, Rhayader, Powys
and printed by MPG Books, Bodmin

Contents

J.M.W. Turner's *View of Hot Well*, c.1800. This feeling of grandeur was lost when the buildings were demolished and rock removed to make navigation of the Avon easier for ships.

HOW THE BOOK CAME ABOUT

The 'Living Memories of Hotwells' Group meet regularly to talk over old times and it was their enthusiasm which gave Hotwells and Cliftonwood Community Association the idea that a photographic exhibition would be a good way to celebrate the millennium. A Lottery Millennium Festival 'Awards for All' grant made everything possible.

At the outset we were warned not to expect a big response to the request for photographs. Nothing could have been further from the truth. Once the word got round, photographs just flooded in (and continue to do so). Every picture tells a story and it has been a great privilege and enormous fun to meet so many people and hear the stories behind their pictures.

It has been an almost impossible task trying to select photographs from nearly 1,000 which were exhibited at Hope Centre in June 2000 in order to tell the story of Hotwells. Sadly many have had to be left out.

The word 'demolished' occurs over and over again in this book. So much so that it would be easy to think that nothing remains of Hotwells and Cliftonwood! Of course that is not so and fortunately the words 'restored', 'renovated' and 'redeveloped' give a more optimistic view.

The word 'flyover' also occurs frequently. This is just a quick way of saying 'The Plimsoll Swing Bridge and road system at Cumberland Basin c. 1960s', which is rather a mouthful.

ACKNOWLEDGEMENTS

Most of the pictures in this book were in the 'Picture Hotwells' exhibition in 2000. We have tried to trace the source of every picture, aware that some were possibly copies. If any copyright claims have been infringed we are very sorry.

Many of these pictures have never been published before and we are very grateful to all the people who so willingly agreed to let us use them in this book:

Bristol City Museum and Art Gallery, The Industrial Museum, Bristol Record Office, Bristol Central Library City Archives.
Margo & Brian Price and Living Memories of Hotwells
John Knott

Mr. M. Tozer
Peter Davey
The Royall Family
Mr. & Mrs. Williams
Jane Purnell
Kathleen Barker
Ruth Edwards
Mr. Tolley
Mrs. Skinner
Valerie Maggs
Peter and Janet Swan
Mrs. Fern Gibbs
Liz and Dave Staples
Mr. Gowan
Kenneth Stradling
The late Audrey Havens
Mark Tucker
The late Mr. E. Davis
Ian Millard
Mr. Shapcott Combes
Hotwells Primary School

John Stops
Denny Long
Mrs. Rafter
Alma Ball
Mr. Jenkins
Father Christopher Hickey
Mr. Maurice Mitchell
Mr. Frank Buckley
Mr. John Buckley
Mr. & Mrs. Stacey
Lone Howell
Pat Crichton, Archivist, Hopetoun House
'Bygone Bristol'
'Memories'
Jem Southam
Derek May
Wendy and Marion Roach
Chris Legge

and the many others who contributed pictures to the exhibition.

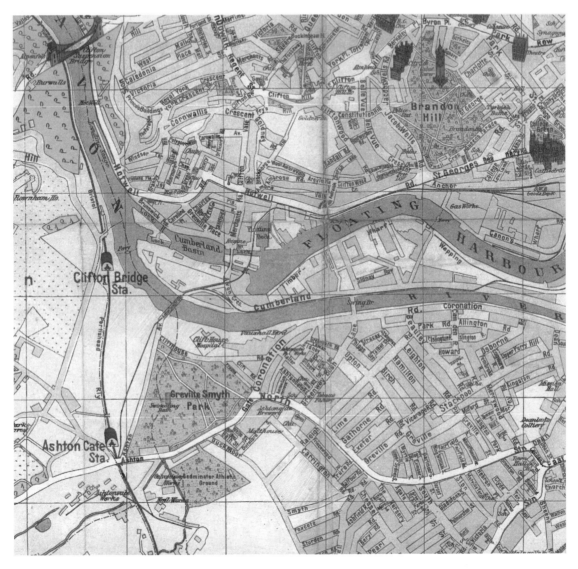

This map from the early 1900s shows the relationship of Hotwells to the Avon, Ashton Park and Gate, Southville, Clifton and Canon's Marsh. It also shows the part of Hotwells lost to the Cumberland Basin flyover. [Ordnance Survey]

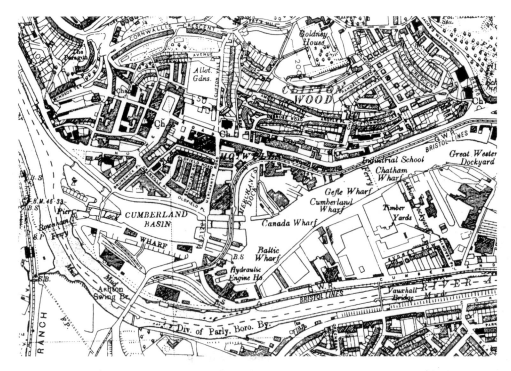

1914 map showing the railway system round the district with names of wharves. [Ordnance Survey]

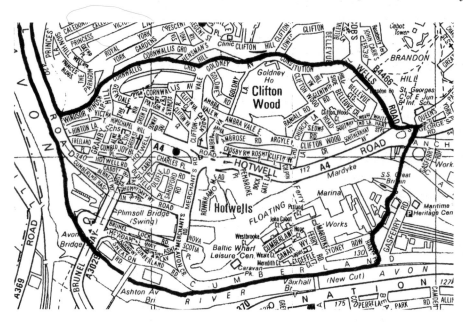

The Hotwells and Cliftonwood district shown on this map is defined by the parish boundary of Holy Trinity, Hotwells. [Geographers A-Z Map Company Ltd]

1 Hotwells before Photography

In winter sometimes, at low tide, you can see a spurt of steam rise from the mudbanks of the Avon under the Suspension Bridge.

This is the last evidence of the phenomenon that gave Hotwells its name: a hot spring that rose from the rock bed of the river. It was first recorded by William Wyrcestre, the Bristol topographer, in the fifteenth century, and Elizabethan sailors used it to treat scurvy. Bristol diamonds mined from the rocks were another Hotwells curiosity that was nationally famous, and 2,000 of them were sent to James I to decorate his palace.

Another famous natural attraction was, of course, the Gorge itself. Visitors from the sixteenth century onwards described it in extravagant romantic terms, comparing it to the Alps, for until the late eighteenth century, the Gorge was narrower and the river banks closer; and the multi-coloured rocks beetled with spectacular crags, from which hung foliage and flowers. Early prints, paintings and engravings of the Hotwell and the Gorge show scenes we can only imagine.

The Gorge is now largely man-made thanks to intensive quarrying, widening of the river banks for road and railways, and above all to the end of sheep grazing, which led to the present dense undergrowth and seeding of trees from Clifton gardens.

But the healing water, the diamonds and the Gorge were for tourists. The fundamental reason for the establishment of this ancient suburb was its position on the Avon, at the first point where at low tide the river could be forded by horse, or crossed by ferry. Right up to the Industrial Revolution, the only other way, if you wanted to get goods over to the Somerset side, was to go into the city and over Bristol Bridge. The Hotwells crossing was vital for centuries, and the earliest record of Rownham ferry is in 1148 when it was owned by the Abbot of St. Augustine's Abbey, who used it to cross to his estate at Abbot's Leigh. Hotwells lay at the gateway to the harbour and Bristol docks, and the area was settled by sailors, ship-builders and dock workers, and remained so until the decline of the City Docks after World War Two.

The Hotwell may have made Hotwells famous, but the spa years were just a rich interlude. Yet the Hotwell did shape the modern suburb, for the architecture survives. The first attempt to commercialise the spring came in 1630 when John Bruckshaw obtained a 40-year lease from the Crown and permission to build a bath house. He put a brick enclosure round the spring, and the waters were boosted by various reports of miraculous cures.

When the lease expired, the Merchant Venturers, who by then owned the land, granted in 1695 a 90-year lease to Charles Jones and Thomas Callow Hill, stipulating that they spent £500 on developing the area for tourists, with a proper pumping system with valves to prevent contamination, lodgings and a bath house, and in 1696, the first Hotwell House was built out of the river itself and the spring.

This was the building that the rich and famous and titled visited in the eighteenth century, having come from the more elegant Bath to the rural delights of Hotwells, with its trips down the river, strawberry teas, and concerts with fireworks. For a few decades, 1760–1790, Hotwells was chic, and Bath and London traders would set up shop in the season which ran from May to October. Hotwell water was bottled and sold in London; hotels, a playhouse and an assembly room were built and locals experienced boom times for once.

Fine terraces and squares were built to lodge the visitors taking the cure: the houses in St. Vincent's Parade, Albemarle Row, Dowry Square, Dowry Parade, Chapel Row, Hope Square and Granby Hill were all designed for letting, and the overflow began to move up to Clifton, then a small rural village with a few grand houses built by prosperous city merchants.

While crowds thronged to the Howell for mainly social reasons, the place flourished but the supposed medicinal properties of the water, which boosted trade, would prove its undoing. As the eighteenth century came to a close, it was the desperate invalids who predominated, and this gave the place a bad name: patients felt they had been sent there to die.

And though huge claims were made for the waters – they would cure gout, the stone, skin disorders, liver and kidney complaints, diabetes, and so on – the most dangerous claim, and the one which damaged the spa most, was that it could cure tuberculosis, or consumption as it was then known. The graves in the Strangers' Burial Ground and in Clifton churchyard soon refuted this, and the medical men, led by Dr. Thomas Beddoes at his Pneumatic Institute in Dowry Square, discounted the water as being of any use.

Then the Napoleonic Wars came, together with an economic crisis and a building slump; the spa movement collapsed, and Hotwells with it. Clifton became the fashionable place to visit instead, and Hotwells went back to being an area that served the docks and the ships, and worked in the associated trades.

The spa did stagger on: the old Hotwell House was demolished in 1822 and a new spa was built by James Bolton, but it never thrived, and in turn was demolished in 1867, along with Hotwell Point, in order to widen the river for shipping. Until the 1930s, Hotwell water was available from a pump in a specially built grotto in the rock, but it was never again taken medicinally.

James Bolton's last-ditch attempt to save the Hot Well Spa failed. Rubble from the demolition work of 1867 was winched up the side of the gorge and used to fill in excavated quarries on the Downs.

The Hot Well Spa was already in decline when this aquatint after J.C. Nattes was published c.1804.

The Overfall Dam near the Floating Harbour and Cumberland Basin: watercolour by T.L. Rowbotham, 1827.

A view of the Hot Well c.1790 showing the Colonnade and the Hotwell House. The tree-lined promenade was designed to give shade to visitors walking to the spa from the lodging houses in Hotwells.

Nineteenth-century illustration from Fanny Burney's *Evelina*, 1792 showing a fine carriage.

15

St Vincent's Rocks with the Hot Well 'from Mr Warren's House' from the south side of the Avon. From *Rocque's Map of Bristol*, 1742.

An etching by Mynde after W. Halfpenny, c.1741, showing the quarry in which the Colonnade was built. The rowing boats were probably manned by Pill hobblers who towed large sailing boats up the Avon to the City Docks.

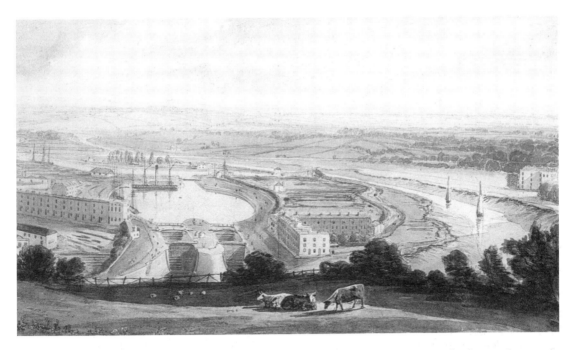

Cumberland Basin c.1828 by Samuel Jackson, who lived for a time at both numbers 3 and 8 Freeland Place, Hotwells. Cumberland Basin was dug out in 1809.

Hotwells from Rownham Hill c.1840 as seen by W.H. Bartlett. People queuing for the ferry can just be seen on the far bank.

A nineteenth-century illustration from *Bristol Diamonds* by Emma Marshall shows well-heeled visitors enjoying music near the Colonnade.

The ever-popular Goldney House grotto, a favourite attraction for visitors to the spa.

The Royal Gloucester Hotel, demolished to make way for the Haberfield almshouses.

The busy Hill's shipyard in 1938. [M.J. Tozer Collection]

A visiting mine-sweeper passes the Rownham Hotel and the bottom of Freeland Place c.1950, before the Plimsoll Bridge was built.

2 The River, the Docks, Ferries and Bridges

Water and the work it provided were the reason why Hotwells developed as a suburb.

The river needed sailors for the ships, dockers to unload them, wharves and warehouses to hold the goods, carters to deliver them, and all those workers needed housing and shops – and pubs – nearby. Over two centuries Hotwells became densely populated.

The Avon has the greatest tidal fall in the world, for twice every 24 hours millions of gallons of water race down the narrow winding channel to the docks, scouring out mud and sewage, and cleaning the entrance to the port at Hotwells.

Or it did until William Jessop, the great docks engineer and designer of the Floating Harbour dammed the course of the Avon at Underfall, and sealed off the dock from the twice-daily scouring of the tide. Because of this, Hotwells often stank of sewage, until Jessop and Brunel solved the problem with culverts and sluices to do what the tide once did. The Underfall today is the last proper working part of the whole system and of special archaeological interest.

The river also provided entertainment, with fishing, sailing, swimming and excursions, even though it was full of sewage well into the mid-twentieth century. In 1822 the Dock Company made a bid to stop "indecent and improper bathing in the harbour", and forbade anyone "to undress himself on shore or expose his naked body to public view". But people still swam in the murky water: until the 1880s, the Leander Swimming Club had an annual race down the New Cut from Bath Bridge to Rownham ferry, despite the fact that the New Cut had several sewage outlets.

The earliest dock at Hotwells was William Champion's wet dock, built in 1765 to take 36 ships: it was bought by the Merchant Venturers in 1770 and became Merchant's Dock, hence the naming of Merchant's Road. New housing now occupies the filled-in site. At the other end of the Mardyke, at the foot of Jacob's Wells Road, was the seventeenth-century Limekiln Dock, filled in at the end of the nineteenth century, and now being excavated for a new housing development.

The famous Anderson
figure-head from the
Demerara.

Shipbuilder Hilhouse had a dock at Hotwells, at Red Clift Yard, by the C tobacco bond building, where he built warships from 1780–1786. Farr's Dock, next door, was opened in 1770, and later became the Hotwell Dock, headquarters of Stotherts. The Cumberland Basin itself was excavated out of the Rownham Meads or fields on the river bend.

The dock built by shipbuilder Charles Hill, a firm which went on working up to the closure of the docks, is still there – the last ship was launched in 1976 – with the dry dock and the *Great Britain* alongside, and now part of the leisure marina by Baltic Wharf, where once the logs came in on Canadian ships and were floated over to the saw mills. Poole's Wharf where coal was landed, is now the site of new housing, as is the Sand Dock.

But while the docks thrived, Hotwells thrived, and the Industrial Revolution brought prosperity and new work to the area, once the Floating Harbour was built in 1802, followed by the New Cut, constructed between 1804 and 1809, and Brunel's new entrance lock scheme, finished in 1849. His swing bridge (still there but never swung nowadays) across the lock, was the first ever to be built with tubular iron sections, and opened in 1840.

Rownham ferry was moved upstream after Brunel's lock was built, and was obviously a profitable crossing, for when the Corporation bought it in 1866, for £10,000, it had carried 150,000 people in the previous six months. It closed in 1933, and at low tide the slipways where the makeshift bridge of boats linked the two banks are still visible.

Until Brunel built his tubular iron bridge which swung across the Cumberland basin lock, the ferry was the only means of getting to the opposite side. By 1853, six ferries were operating between Hotwells and Bath Bridge.

Mardyke ferry, established in 1853 (the Mardyke was named after a Dutch town that Cromwell attacked with two Bristol-fitted ships), took men over to the timber yards, and was opposite the Vauxhall ferry which crossed the New Cut thus linking Hotwells with Ashton and Bedminster. This was a dangerous ferry, for two passengers drowned after the boat drifted into broken water near the Underfall sluice, and in 1900 a swinging footbridge was opened to replace it.

Gas ferry opened in 1830 to take shipbuilders over to work on the *Great Western* and the *Great Britain*, and then was retained for public use, running in all weathers even when the harbour was iced over.

Then, as the Industrial Revolution proceeded and bridge building techniques improved, the traffic shifted; by 1880, 18,000 foot passengers and 2,383 vehicles a day would cross the new Bedminster bridge. Trams could take workers who once went on foot much further afield for work.

With the arrival of dock railways, trains too needed to cross the water, and 1906 saw the opening of Ashton swing bridge, a daring two-decker design, 600-feet long and weighing 1,000 tons, that carried trains on the lower level and people and traffic on the top. It must have caused many delays for in the early 1900s it had to swing at least ten times a day just to let a steamer service from Cardiff through. The last swing was in 1936, when the New Cut more or less closed to shipping, and the bridge itself closed in 1965, after the Cumberland Basin bridge opened.

Another swing bridge nearby was the one by the Nova Scotia pub, opened in 1925, and spanning the only surviving original pre-Brunel dock. It was powered from the Pump House, now a pub, by hydraulic pressure, because it had to operate a big sluice gate as well. The Dock Cottages were built in 1831.

Ironically, the most famous bridge of them all and a landmark for Hotwells, the Suspension Bridge, which opened at last in 1864, did not really affect Hotwells itself, because it mainly served locals living in north Somerset, tourists and the agricultural and farm trade.

Bird's-eye view of the Ashton Swing Bridge, 1906, a double-decker used by trains, cars, carriages and pedestrians. Drawing by Samuel Loxton.

The Mardyke ferry took workers from the Hotwells 'mainland' to work at Charles Hill's yard or one of the many businesses on Spike Island. The ferry closed in 1967.

This view of Cumberland Basin from Rownham Hill, c.1900 shows Clifton Bridge railway station in the foreground.

Seagulls rest on the roof of the RNVR *Flying Fox*. King's tug *Sea Gem* passes in front of a motorised Mardyke ferry, with Cliftonwood in the background, c.1960.

The plight of the *Demerara* in 1851, not the first nor the last vessel to go aground in the Avon, signalled the end of the era when large vessels like Brunel's s.s.*Great Britain* were built in Bristol.

Wood-engraving by Claude FitzHerbert, c.1930 showing tobacco bonds and a ship in the entrance lock.

The new swing bridge in 1906. In 1907/08 it swung an average of 10 times a day.

This view of Cumberland Basin disappeared completely when all these buildings were demolished in the 1960s.

Lady Smythe opening the swing bridge in 1906.

PORT OF BRISTOL AUTHORITY.

NOTICE.

Working of Ashton Swing Bridge on Sundays.

Notice is hereby given that from 1st DECEMBER, 1926, the Ashton Swing Bridge will not be Opened for the Passage of Shipping

On SUNDAYS,

except in cases of emergency, for which application should be made to the Dock and Harbour Master of the City Docks, at Welsh Back, Bristol.

By Order,

D. ROSS-JOHNSON,

General Manager and Secretary.

Docks Office, Queen Square,
Bristol, 26th November, 1926.

The *Birkhalia* went aground in the 'Big Fog' of 1929.

The docks in 1930. Piles of timber and drying sheds can be seen on the right, behind 'Call-out Crescent' (Avon Crescent).

Daedalus, the RNVR ship which preceded the *Flying Fox*, is the only RN vessel whose log records the sighting of a sea-serpent.

Rownham ferry c.1930. At low tide, boats were bridged together to enable the river to be crossed on foot. The slipway can still be seen at low tide.

Limekiln Dock was filled in 1903. The church and brewery, like the dock itself, are long since gone, the area being redeveloped for housing.

The Hallaran family of Hotwells in 1902. The inset picture is of William, drowned when the *Merrimac* went down off Quebec in 1899.

Britannia Buildings, offices of P. & A. Campbell Ltd., owners of the White Funnel Fleet, providing paddle-steamer trips for thousands of Bristolians and visitors.

Mr H.G. Wall at the wheel of this tram outside the Colonnade.

3 Work

For most of its history, work for the people of Hotwells was associated with the river and the docks, and the trades that grew up alongside.

While the women worked as landladies, shop assistants, as servants up in the big houses and hotels in Clifton, or catered for the steamers bringing travellers to the Cumberland Basin landing stages, the men would build ships, haul timber or unload coal or gravel; they made sails and drove the cattle from the cattle boats, sold ship's chandlery, worked the locks, and they worked on dredgers, or on the docks railways, in an area that was teeming with industry and shipping. Hotwells men helped build Brunel's *Great Western* at Pattersons, and the *Great Britain* next door.

There were six shipbuilding docks in the parish: the Merchant's Dock built by William Champion in 1762 for ship repairs and refits and now covered by the Rownham Mead development; the Hotwell Dock, which became the Sand Dock and is now a private marina was developed by shipbuilder James Hilhouse, who took over in 1772 and continued working there until 1823 when he formed a partnership with Charles Hill and opened the Albion Dockyard, which closed only in 1977, though Hills moved their main business to Avonmouth in 1946.

The small Nova Scotia shipyards were active from 1816 to 1903, and shipbuilding on the Mardyke was active from 1793 to 1851. A little further on Limekiln Dockyard, said to date back to 1626, was worked from 1820–1870 when it was taken over by the gas works and eventually filled in for the railway to cross it.

The Hotwell Dock became the home of the Bath engineers, Stotherts, who traded there from 1851 to 1933, and were a major Hotwells employer. The firm, founded in the 1780s, came to Bristol, in 1836, to build steam locomotives for the Great Western Railway.

They went on building locomotives at the Avonside ironworks, but another member of the family, George Kelson Stothert opened a business at Hotwells, where he built some of the earliest iron ships, steamships, engines, and most importantly cranes. One of theirs was shown in the Great Exhibition of 1851,

and four, including the Fairbairn, with its curved jib, can still be seen by the Industrial Museum.

On the banks of the picturesque floating harbour Stotherts had built three ironscrew steamships by 1854, and went on to build steam packets for the Bristol–Newport run, paddle steamers, and tugs big enough to work in the Bristol Channel. The firm continued shipbuilding until 1904, but from then on the business was mainly ship-repairing.

Wooden ships were, of course, still being built throughout the nineteenth century, and the other big employers in Hotwells were the timber merchants who lined Baltic Wharf, now yet another housing development. The only remaining trace of the huge timber trade is in the yard by the *Great Britain* where there are the remains of old drying sheds. The *Great Britain* offices belong to Wickham Norris and the Cottage pub was the waterside office of May and Hassell.

From medieval times, Forest of Dean oak has come in for the shipbuilding trade, followed in the eighteenth century by mahogany, and later, to serve the Victorian building boom, came deal and pine on the big timber sailing ships from Canada and Norway, and sleepers for the new railways.

Much of it came in as logs which were discharged into the water, and poled to the private wharfs, named Gefle, Onega, Cumberland and Canada. It was hard, heavy work, for the cut timber had to be handled on overhead decks from ship to shore and then manhandled down into the drying and seasoning yards behind the waterfront. The timber trade finally left Hotwells in the last decades of the twentieth century.

Other jobs were to be had at the slaughterhouse, in use until the 1950s, on the site of the Rownham Mead development, at McArthurs, the ironfounders, at Holms Sand and Gravel, and on Poole's wharf, hauling coal. Campbell steamers provided plenty of seasonal work.

But once the docks at Avonmouth and Portishead were opened in the late 1870s, to take the big ships that could no longer negotiate the Avon, jobs slowly began to disappear, and Hotwells workers had to look further afield for work.

But the docks-dominated way of life went on until the end of World War Two, with general cargoes coming in to serve the industries in the centre of the city. Wills built their three big redbrick tobacco bonds between 1905 and 1919, and tobacco, cocoa, wine and sherry still came into Hotwells up to the 1950s. It was not until after the closure of the docks, and the building of the Cumberland Basin flyover, that the character of waterside Hotwells really changed.

Now the area is given over to up-market housing developments and leisure pursuits: where the big ships eased their way into the Floating Harbour, there are marinas for yachts, and the boats are replaced by sailboards and canoes. The dredgers left in 1990, and the Pump House's hydraulic engines to work the locks have been replaced by beer pumps.

A few of the old trades survive to serve the leisure industry: boats are still built and repaired, sails stitched and chandlery sold, but all the old heavy industry has gone. Only the Underfall Yard still serves its original purpose, and the Cumberland Basin roads carry the freight that once went by water. Work for Hotwells people now mainly means commuting elsewhere.

Gas company workers laying pipes outside St Vincent's Parade in the 1940s.

Tramways staff.

Diving in the docks. Mr Bennet in the helmet, with Mr Downes of
Hotwells (in cap) lending a steadying hand.

George George, blasting and boring engineer, had the unique task of destroying his own home, Point House, as rock was blasted away to make way for the foundations of the Portway.

Blacksmiths at Stotherts.

Across the river is Poole's Wharf, now a housing development. In the 1940s it was a coal yard.

Bridge master on Ashton swing bridge.

Inside a glass house on the Hotwell Road, watercolour by George Cumberland c.1820. The glass house was in Limekiln Lane. The heat from the furnace was near-intolerable and the workers were unusually well paid.

The *Harry Brown* discharging sand at Sand Wharf, Hotwell Road, in 1978.

John Hurley's ship-breaking business on the banks of the Avon, 1900. Hotwells railway station is in the background.

Opposite, top left: 'Jack of all trades' Albert Roach of Dowry Parade was paid for removing dead bodies from the river: 10 shillings for a person, £1 for cow or horse.

Top right: Mrs Hallaran, midwife. A hundred years ago, mothers could borrow 'lying-in-outfits' from the Clifton Dispensary in Dowry Square.

Bottom: Thousands of hogsheads of tobacco, each weighing over 1,000 pounds, filled the W.D. & H.O. Wills red-brick bonded warehouses around Cumberland Basin. They were not released until the duty had been paid.

Hotwells railway station. [Peter Davey Collection]

4 Transport

Hotwells had an integrated transport system long before the concept existed. In the second half of the nineteenth century, before the motor car arrived, you could travel from Hotwells by water, train, tram or carriage to any part of the city and beyond into the West Country, and indeed to New York!

Travel by horse and by water had gone on since the area was settled; in the eighteenth century visitors to the Hotwell came by carriage along the unmade path that became the Hotwell Road, for sixpence, and could cross on Rownham ferry for a penny. The stage coach stopped at The Bear, which was a coaching inn.

By Victorian times, hackney cabs would take you to Clifton, Kingsdown, the Centre, Queen Square, Redcliffe, and Temple Meads, from the stands at Hotwell House, Cumberland Basin, or Dowry Parade, for fares from one to two shillings. The railway owners realised the importance of linking rail and road services and as early as 1858 the Temple Meads omnibus for Hotwells was running every quarter of an hour.

Or you could get to the Centre or Prince Street by hailing a wherry, a light rowing boat that plied from Underfall "or any stairs" and cost sixpence for one person alone or 3d. each for more than one.

The arrival of a horse-drawn tram service to the Hotwell House in 1880 bought fares down considerably, and the frequency of the service makes modern bus users green with envy. The Hotwell tram to the Centre, Temple Meads and Brislington, cost a penny to threepence, and ran "constantly" from 7.15 am to 11.24 pm; the Tramways Company believed that if the gaps between trams were greater than 12 minutes, people would walk instead.

By 1914, when electric trams had been running on the route to Hotwells since 1900, the service was every five minutes, from 5.35 am to 11.28 pm, and was timed to match the departure and arrival of trains. The last tram from Hotwells left in December 1938 "with a cheery farewell", and motor buses took over.

To get to Long Ashton and Cambridge Batch for 4d. you could take the hourly horse omnibus, later a charabanc, that ran from Trinity Church, from 8.20 am to 9 pm and for Sea Mills and Avonmouth, or Portishead, you took the train, either from the

Albert Roach trying out a penny-farthing bicycle in 1950. The cobbled streets and steep hills of Hotwells and Cliftonwood would have been an enormous challenge.

Hotwell Station, which was near the Suspension Bridge, or from the Clifton Bridge Station, reached by Rownham Ferry.

The Port and Pier Railway opened in 1865, anticipating the shift of dock trade to Avonmouth. It entailed building 500 yards of tunnel under Bridge Valley Road, and in 1874, it linked up with the Clifton Extension line, and thus the rest of the suburban stations.

By 1893, this train, whose terminus was by the Suspension Bridge, delivered passengers to the Hotwells tram, the Rocks Railway, and thence to the Suspension Bridge, the Rownham ferry, the hackney stand or the landing stage for departures by ship. It was a comprehensive transport system that modern Bristol can only dream of.

This line closed with the building of the Portway, which opened in 1926 and marked a shift from rail to road transport of goods. But it had one more role to play, as we shall see, during the Blitz.

The other railway line, the Bristol and Portishead running along the Somerset side of the Gorge, was opened in 1867, and linked Portishead and its dock with Ashton, and thence, via the docks railway, the city docks; it was a freight and passenger line that fell into disuse in the 1970s, and is now restored as a freight line only, ironically to transport cars coming in at Portbury Dock.

Departure by water came naturally to Hotwells, and up to World War Two it was the gateway literally to the world. At Cumberland Basin you could embark on one of the dozens of shipping lines with routes not just to the coastal ports of the Bristol Channel, but Liverpool, Cork, le Havre, Bordeaux, Rotterdam, Hamburg, and New York. Severn trows also took passengers to the Severn and thence the Midlands.

These services ran twice weekly or twice monthly, but you could catch a passenger steamer to Cardiff every day, and after 1887, for "marine excursionists", came the Campbell pleasure steamers, offering trips to Wales and north Devon. While the big passenger boats moved to Avonmouth, the steamers stayed and still make special excursions occasionally, on the restored paddle steamer *Waverley* (once known as "the greyhound of the Bristol Channel") and the *Balmoral*, though no longer from the specially-built and now rotting landing stage by St. Vincent's Parade.

From there between 1893 and 1934, trippers could ride up the steep side of the Gorge on the Clifton Rocks Railway (a penny up, halfpenny down) and go on to the Suspension Bridge or the Zoo. The Rocks Railway was built with a spa revival in mind, for publisher George Newnes wanted to pump up the Hotwell water to establish a hydropathic centre at what is now the Avon Gorge Hotel.

A Bristol bi-plane flying over Hotwells, c.1900.

The funicular railway, built with great difficulty inside a 500-foot tunnel in the rock, was hydraulic, and the blue and white cars, nervous passengers were assured, "gripped the rails with a vice-like tenacity". Initially the Lift, as it was called, was very popular, not only with tourists but with Hotwells people who worked up in Clifton, but in the long term it never made much profit, and the arrival of the Portway and the motor car finished it off by 1934.

Until 1926, when the Portway opened, Bridge Valley Road was the end of the line on the Gloucestershire side, and people were not entirely happy at the change. "The pleasant footpath that runs to Sea Mills will be a wide thoroughfare noisy with trams and motors, something will be lost and the riverside will no longer be the same," wrote Arthur Salmon in 1922.

Clifton Rocks from Leigh Woods, Bristol. 651.

Direction of the Rocks Railway. [both pictures: Peter Davey Collection]

The Rocks Railway being dismantled in 1934.

The entrance in 1912. [Peter Davey Collection]

A passenger train travelling along the Mardyke on Hotwell Road.

Clifton Bridge railway station on the Somerset side of the river.

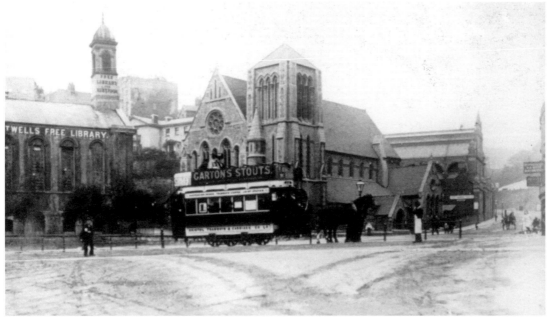

A horse-drawn tram at the bottom of Jacob's Wells Road near St Peter's church, the Hotwells Free Library and Jacob's Wells swimming pool.

P. & A. Campbell's steamship *Devonia*. Clifton National School is to the left at the top of the hill with, below, the Industrial School (until 1845 this was the local work-house).

The *Devonia* (right) serving as a mine-sweeper camouflaged for Second World War work. She was one of seven Campbell paddle-steamers which helped in the Channel evacuation from northern France in 1940, but was badly damaged and abandoned.

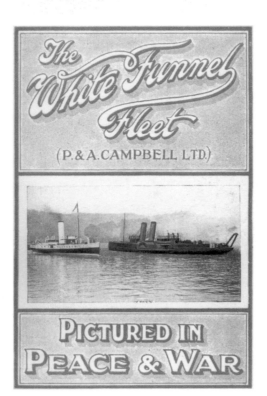

Between-the-wars tram outside the recently built Hillsborough flats. [Peter Davey Collection]

Trips by Taxicab and Private Cab.

Early twentieth-century luxury travel.

Rate of Charges for the half-day (8 hours) : 25s. for the first 25 miles and 7½d. per mile for every mile above 25 miles.

Rate of Charges for the whole day (up to 16 hours) : 50s. for the first 50 miles and 7½d. per mile for every mile above 50 miles.

Mr Rice ran a well-stocked hardware shop in the premises recently occupied by Marcruss Stores.

5 Shops and Shopkeepers

Once upon a time you could shop till you dropped in the Hotwell Road. There were continuous shops from Anchor Road to Dowry Square, on both sides.

So why did almost all of them disappear?

Road widening in 1865 and in the 1880s removed some, as did slum clearance on the Clifton Wood slopes, and the demolition of Love Street in the 1930s to build the Hillsborough flats. The arrival of trams enabled people to shop in cheaper Castle Street and in the markets, and the gradual decline of the city docks meant some of the population moved out to Avonmouth and Portishead.

New council housing elsewhere in the city took more residents away, and the Depression drove some shops out of business. Refrigerators removed the need to shop daily, and the first supermarket chains undercut local shop prices. Though the population of Hotwells since the 1970s has increased, the number of shops goes on shrinking, and the goods they sell are strikingly different. Only the pubs endure . . .

The decline was gradual, for even in 1964 Hotwells still had 26 shops, including a chemist, a wine merchant, a fishmonger and a draper. At the time of writing, we are down to fewer than a dozen shops, despite the re-development and upgrading of the area. Thank the motor car for that.

Even as early as 1775, there were over a hundred Hotwells traders listed in the city directory, if you include publicans and landlords, there to serve both local residents and visitors to the fashionable spa. Local people doubled as landlords and shop-keepers, but retailers in Bath and even London came in the season to open shops selling luxuries such as wigs, perfume and lace. Haberdashery, tailoring, millinery and shoes were also on sale to wealthy visitors.

Spa souvenirs were another profitable line, and this trade went on well into the nineteenth century, for James Bolton sold toothpowder, fancy articles in lava, boomerangs, fossils, oiled silk caps and respirators, portable seats, soap, and knife-cleaning machines. Earlier, visitors could find nearby a circulating library, an umbrella-maker, a miniature painter, a coach-maker and watchmaker. The Gloucester Hotel, the Lebeck

Tavern, the Stork and the York Hotel provided meals, and pubs that survive over two centuries later are the Adam and Eve, the Bear, the Spring Gardens and the Plume of Feathers.

The eighteenth-century Hotwellians had all the trades and shops needed: carpenter, saddler, poulterer, confectioner, wine and spirit merchant, draper, grocer, tea dealer, and a baker and a butcher, although many shoppers would buy food in the markets on Welsh Back and at Bristol Bridge.

As the suburb grew, the shops multiplied, and by 1879 there were, incredibly, 194 small businesses operating – plus 32 pubs – and they stayed open mostly until midnight. Every need was met: there were dozens of grocers, butchers, bakers and greengrocers, each serving a small local community. When money was tight and there was nowhere to store food, people shopped daily.

There were tobacconists, refreshment rooms, drapers, tobacconists, newsagents, second-hand furniture shops, two pawnbrokers, undertakers, several boot and shoemakers, laundries, hairdressers, coal and oil merchants, and chemists. There was a public library in the former St. Peter's Church on the Anchor Road roundabout, from 1888 to 1905.

By 1915, Hotwells even had a branch of Lloyds Bank, a cinema, and a tiny department store in the shape of Axtens, the drapers, the biggest concern on the Hotwell Road. They operated from the 1880s until the 1940s.

A breakdown of the shops during World War One shows there were still ten butchers, nine confectioners, six bootmakers, six second-hand shops, eight grocers, five hairdressers, seven tailors and drapers, five fried fish shops, seven tobacconists, two dairies and five refreshment rooms. The pub count was down to a mere 17! There were also two doctors, a dentist, a stationer and a bookshop, all signs of a settled community.

All these Hotwells businesses were small family concerns; the owners or tenants usually lived over the shop and sometimes two businesses were run from the same premises. Often the wives ran the shop and the husband worked in the docks. These businesses came and went, but a few shops were passed on through the generations, as the photographs prove. Several generations of the Davis family ran their newsagent business at 255 Hotwell Road, and Royalls, founded in 1924, was one of the first Spar shops in Britain.

Great-grandfather Royall worked on the laying of the Portway, was run over by a steam roller and left just £30 to his eight sons; Bill bought a horse and cart and a load of apples and sold them at Severn Beach and gradually made enough profit to open the shop at 275 Hotwell Road.

Right up to World War Two, as the Royall amateur map shows, shopping in Hotwells was vibrant. "On Saturday night, from 6 pm onwards, Trinity to the Mardyke was really busy, with people shopping up to 10 pm. Everyone lived on the premises and people knocked on the door if they wanted anything. They sent kids with a note saying 'Let Dolly have 2 ozs. ham and four rashers, pay you tomorrow'. On Christmas Eve it would be near midnight when you closed. You could buy everything you needed from the cradle to the grave – baby-clothes, wedding dresses and even a coffin."

Hotwell Road, showing the bustling commercial life that would survive until the 1950s.

SHOPPING ON THE HOTWELL ROAD IN THE 1930s
as remembered by Ken Royall

The only pubs named are those which give the reader a point of reference.   There were a great many!

Starting along Love Street from Dowry Square.

YORK HOTEL
OSMOND BROS. MOTOR REPAIRS
MR. BILL NELMES, FRIED FISH SHOP
MR. TOOL' S, (DAIRYMAN) STABLE FOR HIS HIGH STEPPING HORSE
MR. SONNY PORTER, FRESH FISH AND POULTRY.
 MR. TOM ADAMS , CHIMNEY SWEEP
MR. FEAR, WATCH AND CLOCK REPAIRS
MR. & MRS. MUTTER, GROCERS.
MAISON GUISE, LADIES HAIRDRESSER.
LLOYDS BANK (ON CORNER OF CLIFTON VALE)

Nearly all the above businesses were demolished when Hillborough Flats were built in the mid 1930s.

From the Chuch to the road up to Ambra Vale

MARRIOT'S PORK BUTCHER
BAPTIST CHURCH
HOTWELLS CINEMA
ROBINSON'S REMOVALS OFFICE AND YARD
TAYLOR'S BAKERY AND CAKE SHOP

Church Steps

SPEED'S NEWSAGENTS
MARDYKE HOTEL.

Cross Hotwell Road to retrace steps

FLYING FOX RNVR VESSEL
MR. HODGE, BUTCHER
POOLE'S WHARF - COALYARD.
CATES - UNDERTAKER.
2 UNKNOWN SHOPS
PEARK'S GROCERY AND PROVISIONS
MR. RICE, IRONMONGER
KNOWLES (TOP SHOP) GROCERS
BILL TUCKER, FRUIT AND VEG.
SHORE AND SULLIVAN , PAWNBROKERS AND JEWELLERS
MR. AND MRS. JAMES   FRIED FISH SHOP

MACE, CONFECTIONER WITH A VERY ATTRACTIVE SHOP WINDOW
A BRANCH OF VICTORIA WINES.
AXTENS A BIG STORE WITH 3 SHOP WINDOWS AND 2 ENTRANCES
HARRY EVANS, NEWSAGENT
EASTMAN'S, BUTCHERS
MR. PIBWORTH, TAILOR
TAYLERS, FAMILY BUTCHER
MR. JENNINGS, CHEMIST AND POS OFFICE
PARISH'S, FAMILY BUTCHER
STEAM PACKET   PUB

Merchant's Road

KNOWLES GROCERS AND HARDWARE MANAGED BY MR. SAGE
MILTON'S CAKE SHOP
THE TRINITY ROOMS

Into Love Street opposite Hillsborough

MISS ALWAYS, FLORIST , FRUIT AND VEG.
MR. DERRICK, BARBER
A SMALL SLAUGHTERHOUSE BESIDE WHAT IS NOW BRENDA'S.
COURTNEY'S BUTCHER'S SHOP. (THEY OWNED THE SLAUGHTERHOUSE)
HARDING'S BUTCHERS
TED DAVIS, NEWSAGENT
HODDER'S CHEMIST SHOP
BEAR HOTEL AND ENTRANCE TO BEAR GARAGE
THE NEXT FOUR HOUSES WERE ALTERED TO ACCOMMODATE THE NEW FISH
AND CHIP SHOP FOR MR. AND MRS. NELMES.
ON THE CORNER OF DOWRY PARADE WAS THE ENTRANCE TO MR. DOWN'S
GROCER.
THE DOWRY HOTEL.

Both the Hotel and Grocers were demolished when the entrance to Love Street was widened.   The three story building put up at this time became ROYALL'S GROCERS.

The demolition of so many businesses in Love Street to enable Hillsborough Flats to be built sounded the death knell for the 'Hotwells Shopping Centre of the 30s' and it was downhill all the way from that time to the present when hopefully, there will be a resurgence of new businesses to meet the demands of the many new residents.

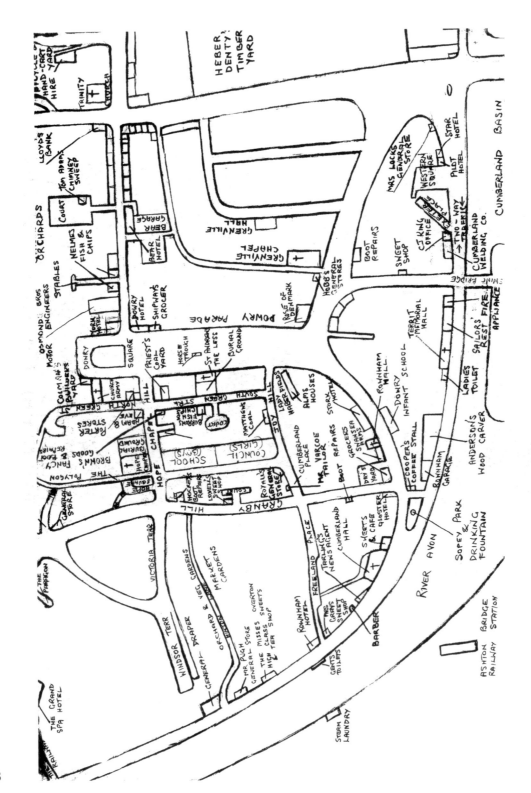

58

Hotwells and Lower Clifton c.1930: drawn from memory by the late Ken Royall.

The Colonnade provided shops for visitors to the Hot Well spa.

Love Street, Hotwells around 1910. The greengrocer's on the right is on the
site of Hillsborough flats at the bottom of Clifton Vale.

Love Street around 1900 with Hotwell Road in the distance. Hillsborough
flats now to the left.

The diminutive Harry Evans was often hidden by the piles of newspapers on his shop counter.

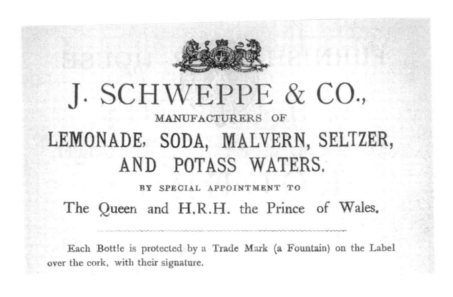

Schweppes had premises in Dowry Square.

62

Mr Pugh owned a general store at the bottom of Hinton Lane between the wars: a handy last-stop for passengers joining a steamer trip.

The first Davis newsagent's shop c.1911, on Hotwell Road where Hillsborough flats now stand.

The second Davis shop, on the other side of the road, in 1916. The cheeky postcards in the window were either to cheer people up in difficult times, or featured famous music-hall stars.

The Royall family in 1974, having served Hotwellians for 50 years.

Brownes tea-rooms were established next to the Nova Scotia in 1906, closing in 1973. From 1952 the business was run by Marjorie and Leslie Williams, famous for the four and a half thousand hot-cross buns they made at Easter.

Ellen and Rolinda Sharples. Paintings by Rolinda can be seen in the city's art gallery. She died at number 3 St Vincent's Parade, outlived by her mother, whose generosity led to the founding of the Royal West of England Academy.

6 Hotwells Notables

In the eighteenth century, when the Hotwell was a noted spa, the famous and the titled flocked to Hotwells, but very few of them actually lived there, although the suburb did become home to some famous and infamous folk.

Rolinda Sharples (1793–1838), the artist, lived at 3 St. Vincent's Parade and unusually for a woman made a living from her work, thanks to the careful training provided by her practical mother, Ellen, the benefactress who gave money and paintings for the founding of what was to become the Royal West of England Academy. Rolinda specialised in portraits and crowd scenes and some of her work can be seen at Bristol Museum and Art Gallery. Her famous contemporary, Samuel Jackson, also lived in Hotwells for some years, at 3 and 8 Freeland Place.

Another Hotwells artist is famous for another reason. Frederick Hiles was one of the Hotwells children who tried to get a free ride by jumping on to the back of the trams. Eight year-old Frederick fell into the path of an oncoming tram and both his arms had to be amputated at the shoulder. He was determined to become an artist, and he learned to hold the brush in his mouth, changed his first name to Bartram and, at 16, exhibited at the Bristol Academy of Fine Arts (later the RWA), and then studied in Paris.

He returned to Hotwells in 1906, and lived in a small house in Constitution Hill, where he earned his bread and butter designing postcards for Raphael Tuck. He painted hundreds of pleasant and accomplished local landscapes which occasionally turn up at auctions today. But he had developed severe gum disease, from holding the brushes in his mouth, and died in 1927, aged 55.

A living artist who was directly inspired by Hotwells, and more particularly, its mud, is Richard Long RA, (1945–), whose installations are in major galleries (including, of course, Bristol) all over the world. He played by the river, in and on it, and experimented with mud to make patterns and shapes and imprints; he still uses bucket-loads to make a wall painting of swirling figures and patterns. His love of the natural materials of the landscape have taken him on long solitary walks all over

Hannah More
1745-1833.

'Milk-maid poet'
Ann Yearsley.

the globe, for much of his art is made by altering the landscape by leaving some impermanent mark, a circle of stones in a stream for example, photographing it and writing a caption, a kind of diary note on the time, the place, the light and the mood.

On the literary front, it was a Hotwells woman who caused the famous Bristol writer Hannah More a great deal of annoyance and publicity. Ann Yearsley (1752–1806), the milkmaid poet, who lived in poverty in Clifton, was taken up by the philanthropic More, who prepared a volume of her poems, found a thousand subscribers and in 1785 got a book published. It sold well and the money raised, some £350, a very large sum for those days, was meant to help the impoverished Yearsley family.

Ann, an independent spirit, resented having the money managed for her, and wanted to spend it as she thought fit. The two women had a ferocious argument, and society was divided into two camps, but Yearsley got her way, and with some of the money, opened a circulating library at the Colonnade next to the Hotwell House. She went on to write a play, *Earl Godwin*, which had a few performances at the Bath and Bristol theatres. She died, still nursing a grudge, at Melksham, her work completely forgotten.

The same could be said of Hannah More (1745–1833) herself, who lived in the area only in her old age, when she moved from Wrington to 4 Windsor Terrace, where she died.

She had been a teacher, successful playwright, with hits in London, Bristol and Bath, a poet, a novelist, an expert on education, a tract writer, a philanthropist, a campaigner against slavery, a social reformer who bettered the lot of the urban and rural poor by starting schools, including one in Bristol's Park Street, and a blue-stocking friend of the influential and famous.

Nowadays her work seems patronising and high-minded, but in her day she was idolised for her good works and fine mind. She also was a tremendous earner; she is estimated to have made £40,000 from her writing, the equivalent of millions today.

When, in 1828, she came to Windsor Terrace, to the house owned by Dr. Whalley (who found it too damp to live there), she was in poor health, and lived there quietly until her death, with her companion, Mary Frowd, receiving the odd visit from her famous friends, including William Wilberforce. She left £30,000, much of it to Bristol charities.

Dr. Thomas Beddoes (1760–1808) was famous too, for rather different reasons: he was a medical doctor and scientist interested in gases, and did controversial experiments from 1793 to 1799 at his first makeshift laboratory at 11 Hope Square, and set up his Pneumatic Institute at 6 Dowry Square in 1799.

He had come to Hotwells deliberately in search of consumptives to treat with his new cure, nitrous oxide, delivered in an airbag. He also treated his patients with cows' breath, by shutting them in a curtained chair, and poking the cow's head inside. He was the famous discoverer with his employees – Humphry Davy and Peter Roget, later of *Thesaurus* fame – of nitrous oxide, or laughing gas, later used as the first modern anaesthetic, though he and his literary friends, including Coleridge and Southey, used it to get high and prance along the Hotwell Road to the Avon, "laughing and tingling in every toe and finger-tip".

Dr Thomas Beddoes.

The Pneumatic Institute flourished at first but by 1801 it was obvious that the Beddoes cure did not work; and the establishment closed. Beddoes went to live up in Clifton, and died in 1808. He is buried in the Strangers' Burial Ground alongside the many patients who died from the disease he tried to cure. And near his old Institute in 1912 came another man concerned with cures, Joseph Schweppe, who set up in Dowry Square to sell digestive soda water "impregnated with air".

Another spa connection is James Johnson, a renowned fossil collector who lived at 12 Dowry Parade and built up an amazing collection in the early part of the nineteenth century. When sold, much of it went to The Bristol Institution, the forerunner of the Bristol City Museum, but sadly many of the fossils were destroyed in the Blitz.

Humphry Davy.

Lady Hope left Hotwells an amazing legacy: a chapel, a schoolroom and a square all named after her. She had come with her friend Lady Glenorchy to take the waters at the Hotwell and wanted their chapel to be near the spa, where they were treated for consumption. They were strongly evangelical, and together financed the building of the chapel that Lady Hope did not live long enough to see opened in 1787.

John Anderson, ships' carver, came to Hotwells in 1865 to join his uncle at his studio on the Hotwell Road; they made figureheads that became famous Bristol landmarks, like the one for the *Demerara*, and were so skilled that churches employed them, too, to carve cherubs and angels.

In the 1890s, when wooden ships were mostly replaced by iron and figureheads were no longer needed, he turned to carving fairground horses, and figures to stand outside shops. Anderson roundabout horses were nationally admired and sought after. Arthur Ernest Anderson inherited the business in 1913 and it closed in 1931 when he died. The firm's tools and examples of their work can be seen in the Industrial Museum.

Howells even had its own giant, Patrick Cotter, or O'Brien, who lived his final years in Hotwells. His skeleton in the museum of Trinity College, Dublin measures 7 ft 1 in, though he was credited with being much taller in his youth.

Robert Southey.

Samuel Taylor Coleridge.

The Pneumatic Institute in the corner of Dowry Square where Humphry
Davy and friends had fun experimenting with laughing gas.

He was born in 1760 and worked as a bricklayer until a showman purchased him from his parents for £10 and brought him to Bristol in 1779 to go on show. He then moved on to London to be exhibited at fairs and theatres.

Cotter returned to Bristol in 1783 to go on show at the Full Moon Inn at Stokes Croft, and he finally settled for good in a lodging house at Hotwells in 1804, where he caused alarm by lighting his pipe from the street oil lamps; it was said that being too big to sit in a chair, he usually sat on a table and rested his arm over the top of a door.

He died in 1806 and was buried in the Jesuit Chapel in Trenchard Street, in a coffin measuring nine feet two inches, and was buried in rock in an attempt to prevent the anatomists from digging him up. His shoes, spectacles and walking stick ended up in Blaise Museum, and the chair made for him to use at his pub, the long gone Old Lion, was auctioned off. His bones were exhumed several times and it was established that he suffered from acromegaly, a disease where the bones grow too fast.

Sam Tucker and Harold Jarman were two sporting greats who came from Hotwells. Sam was a stevedore at the Port of Bristol and played for Bristol Rugby Club (as later did another Hotwellian, Mike Rafter) and captained the England team. Sam was so famous that his portrait was used on the tissue wrappers for oranges.

Harold Jarman began his football career with the Hotwells Boys Club and in 1959 joined Bristol Rovers, for whom he played until the 1970s. He became a cult hero and fans used to chant "Harold, Harold", when he appeared at Eastville Stadium. Jarman later became the only Bristolian to manage Rovers, and he was also a fine cricketer, playing for Gloucestershire between 1961 and 1971.

In the modern world of the arts, Hinton Lane can boast a hell-raising Peter O'Toole who lived there when he had his first engagement at the Bristol Old Vic; Moira Shearer lived in Dowry Parade for a while. Blackadder aka Tony Robinson, lived just inside the parish boundary, in Glendale, and children's author Diana Wynne Jones settled in the Polygon. Fred Wedlock married a Hotwellian and owns a rare surviving bottle of Hotwell spa water. The film character, Morph, was created at Stork House by the team that was to become Aardman Animation.

Some of the names of streets still commemorate famous inhabitants or visitors; Cumberland, Albemarle and Cornwallis were generals, the Marquis of Granby visited in 1744, and subscribed to Dowry Chapel. The Rose of Denmark was Alexandra, wife of Edward VII, Samuel Plimsoll saved ships from dangerous overloading with his famous Line, but didn't live in the area. Sir John Kerle Haberfield was an alderman and Lord Mayor and his wife endowed the almshouses in 1891, and Dr. Carrick was a physician at the spa. The vanished Caroline Place was named after the wife of George IV.

Patrick Cotter (or O'Brien) was the celebrated giant who lived in Hotwells. His shoes, spectacles and walking stick ended up in Blaise Museum. He died in 1806.

Ruby (12) and Elsie Brown (3) were thrown from Clifton Suspension Bridge into the river (a fall of 245 feet) in September 1896. They were rescued from the water by James Hazell, boatman.

The Glorious Gloucestershire Regiment marching over the Ashton Bridge and past 'B' Bond during the First World War. The song was one remembered by Vernon Gay.

James Griffin, a tram-car conductor who lost his life trying to save
Caroline Bryant at Hotwells on June 6th, 1906.

Children of Camden Terrace, c.1950: Carol Tool, Christine and Carol Porter, John Mead, Phyllis Brooks, Diane James, Jane and Susan Wiltshire.

William and Edward Shapcott Coombs of 332 Hotwell Road, c.1910.

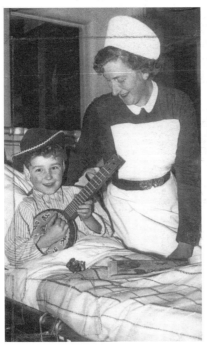

Mike Rafter recovered from a stay in hospital and went on to play rugby for England.

The Holes who lived at the bottom of Jacob's Wells Road, c.1890.

77

Mr Jenkins, company secretary of Campbell's, and resident of Dowry Parade, pictured with his family.

Florence Brown receiving a gold pen in 1963 to mark her becoming the first woman Lord Mayor of Bristol.

Mrs Payne and Kath Barker
wearing Easter bonnets in the
Merchants public house.

Another wonderful hat: Dorothy
May Andrews, c.1920s.

Dr Hickey, concerned for all
who were genuinely ill in
Hotwells, but who had no
sympathy with 'shirkers'.

Photograph of Eliza Johnston
with Millie and John taken by
Henry Johnston, a founder-
member of Bristol Photographic
Society. They lived in Sandford
Road, around 1900.

Sydney and Dolly Evans at 292 Hotwell Road, c.1910 in one of the houses demolished to widen the Portway.

Albert McGrath was a great character who loved Hotwells and lived in Lebeck House. This was pulled down to be replaced by the Carrick House flats.

Tennis courts in the quarry along the Portway, 1930s.

7 Leisure and Entertainment

For most Hotwellians, before World War Two, leisure and entertainment meant two places, the pub and the chapel.

They were the main social centres for the area, and a welcome escape from work and drudgery at home. They provided friendship, entertainment, enlightenment and relaxation in a pre-television age.

But in the eighteenth century, Hotwells had become one big entertainment area, thanks to the spa. Visitors would attend balls, and banquets in the Royal Gloucester Hotel (site of Haberfield almshouses) whose trade card boasted "a good and well-supplied larder with Turtle in season, with Dinners, Suppers, hand-made dishes and Soups sent out at the shortest notice" – take-away is not a new idea – "and Stabling with good lock-up coach houses." After dinner, guests could stroll in the New Vauxhall Gardens, whose whereabouts are uncertain.

These elaborate pleasure gardens, complete with bowling green and supper room, opened in 1743, and 2,000 people turned up to celebrate. There were fireworks, music played from boats on the water, trips down the river at night, and across the Avon, strawberry teas at Long Ashton. In the evenings the fashionable crowd could go to a concert in the Long Room, a soirée at the New Room, or to a play at the Jacob's Wells Theatre, which was opened by Somerset actor John Hippisley in 1728 and enlarged in 1747.

This theatre, which Chatterton called a hut, was next to an alehouse, so drink could be passed in through a hole in the wall, and there were frequent fights and pickpockets awaited the audience afterwards as they crossed Brandon Hill. The programme was mixed, with low comedies, Shakespeare, Congreve and pantomime. The little theatre finally closed in 1771, killed off by the arrival of the superior Theatre Royal. It was demolished in 1803, and the upper block of flats in Jacob's Wells Road stands on the site.

But all these facilities were for visitors, not locals: their sport was to gape at the antics of the rich and famous patrons of the Hotwell, and then retire to the alehouse; the Plume of Feathers,

The Bear, the Adam and Eve all date from the eighteenth century and survivors from the early nineteenth century are The Mardyke, The Spring Gardens, The Nova Scotia, The Rose of Denmark and The Merchants Arms.

Hotwells was famous for its pubs, of which there were once 32 in one mile, and there were other premises licenced to sell ale, so it is not surprising that middle-class Clifton focused its temperance efforts on Hotwells. But the pub served a useful role, as an escape from cramped poor housing; for a few pence you could forget the hard work and the poverty for an hour or two.

For the women, the escape was not the pub but chapel, which provided almost all the social life of women and children. They went to several services on Sundays, the children to Sunday school, and in the week there were sing-songs, sewing bees, entertainments, and of course, once a year, the Outing.

The slow decline of Hope Chapel, down to a congregation of three by the time it became a community centre in the 1970s, mirrors the experience of all the chapels: gradually they became redundant and were demolished, or their use was changed. Only Trinity Church survives, though Hope Chapel has now been reclaimed for religious worship.

It was not that Hotwells became godless, but that the population declined, thanks to slum clearance, and those left became better off and more mobile. With the arrival of public transport, people could seek a social life outside the area. They could hire bicycles, or afford to go on steamer trips, and after 1915 they could go to the Hotwells Cinema, which stood near the Spring Gardens pub.

There, to demon piano accompaniment by Miss Viola Jukes, they could watch silent films such as *The Canker of Jealousy*. The cinema seated 450, prices were 3d., 4d. and 6d., and the place was furnished in luxurious style with tip-up chairs, upholstered in red velvet, according to the opening announcement.

There were two showings a day, every day including Christmas, and matinees for children, who like kids everywhere at Saturday morning cinema, threw "pinky" (rotten) fruit at the screen until the manager threatened to stop the show. Literate children would get in free if they found an adult who needed the subtitles read to him.

"We used to go to the cinema with my grandfather, Harry Rex, and as we walked along the Hotwell Road, other kids would join us. He couldn't read and whoever sat next to him had to tell him what was on the captions. On the way out the manager would often stop grandfather and say, 'there's half a dozen kids going in on your name tonight.' He didn't know who they were but he always paid up like a lord," remembered Marjorie Palmer. Sadly, there is no photograph of the cinema, which closed in 1940, after bomb damage.

But Hotwells never had a proper performing space. In North Green Street there was the Albert Hall, recently converted into flats; it held 300, and was used mainly for youth activities, but there was nowhere for sports events, nowhere to put on plays or music hall entertainments.

The YMCA tried to fill the gap when in 1908 they opened the Hotwells Adult School club, which had a skittle alley, billiards, a games room, a refreshment bar, a wash-house and a big space for plays, debates and indoor sports; Hope Centre took over this community role in the 1970s and flourished for over 20 years.

Nor did Hotwells ever have a public park: there were a few public spaces, like Sopey Park at the bottom of Granby Hill, and allotments at Cabbage Gardens, but the main playground had to be the waterfront. If Hotwells people wanted to play football or cricket they would go to Ashton Park, Greville Smythe Park or Seamills. The only municipal provision in Hotwells itself was at Jacob's Wells, where from 1888 to 1905 there was a public library in a redundant church, and the swimming and slipper baths, opened nearby in 1884.

Ironically, in the twenty-first century with the re-development of the waterside, modern Hotwells is now becoming a leisure area for the whole city.

Holy Trinity Football Club 1914–15.

Hotwells Primary School football team 1968.

The original Hotwells Boys' Club photographed outside the Albert Hall, North Green Street in 1939. The club was mixed until the girls moved to Holy Trinity.

The Lord Mayor visited the club in 1942.

Betty Davis, in one of Edie Ryan's Dancing Shows at the Albert Hall,
North Green Street c.1929.

Kathleen Cook as the May Queen at the Band of Hope celebrations 1935/36 with Ruth Edwards as the train-bearer and Ken Jenkins carrying the cushion.

Coronation celebrations behind the Spring Gardens pub in 1937, when Violet Payne was the landlady. This terrace was destroyed by enemy bombs.

A 1920s outing from Hotwells was always a treat, whatever the weather.

The *Merrimac* pleasure-steamer by the Hotwells slip was originally built as a tug-boat but converted to an excursion vessel to Chepstow.

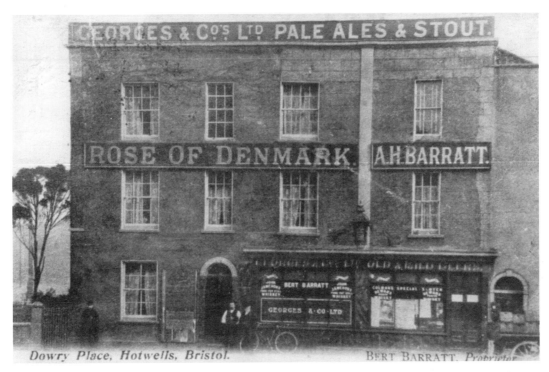

A great survivor: one of Hotwells' popular old pubs.

The Pump House pub was created out of the old Hydraulic Engine House of 1870.

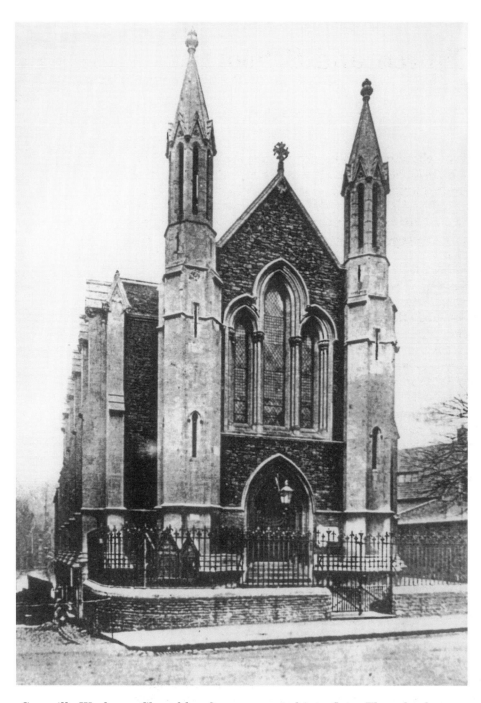

Grenville Wesleyan Chapel has been converted into flats. The school-room, once the home of Hotwells Boys' Club, is now home to Bristol Bridge Club.

8 Church and School

Compulsory education for all children up to the age of 13 came into force in 1870: at that time it was estimated that a third of Bristol children aged five to 12 were not on any school register. Before that Hotwells children might get a basic three R's education at a cheap dame school, or an "academy"; the directory for 1861 lists two schools for ladies on Granby Hill, and one for boys in the Polygon.

Most parents had to rely on the board or national schools: Clifton National School opened in 1812, near what had been the workhouse on the Clifton Wood slope above Mardyke, and children would go there until economic forces meant they had to start work.

When schooling became compulsory in 1870, numbers went up, so some Hotwells children then attended Christ Church school in Clifton in what is now the library in Princess Victoria Street or the Lower Belle Vue School on Jacob's Wells, as well as the old Clifton National School, which eventually moved from Mardyke to the old Long Room on the waterfront, where visitors to the spa had once had banquets and dances, until a new school could be built.

When the Clifton Hotwells School, now Hotwells Primary, built to house the extra pupils, opened on Hope Chapel Hill in 1877, the nursery and infant sections stayed in the Long Room, which was used as a school well into the 1930s; this was demolished in 1963, when the Cumberland Basin flyover was being built.

There was also a Dowry Branch School for infants, in Dowry Square, and another Infant School, founded in 1912, later to become Trinity Infant National School, at the Trinity Rooms, where the church had its Sunday School. Finally, all the various schools were amalgamated to form Hotwells Primary School, run by the LEA.

Until the local councils and the state took over provision, education was frequently supplied by the churches and chapels. Each denomination ran a Sunday School where as well as bible studies, reading, writing and numbers were taught, and domestic skills for girls. All these church Sunday schools had respectable libraries.

The Simon Short fountain commemorated a gentleman who championed seamen and who was associated with the Bethel ship – a floating ministry to seamen. Erected in the park at the bottom of Granby Hill in 1902, it is now sited by the Old Trinity Rooms.

The fact that Hope Chapel built such a large schoolroom next door is witness to the need, and in 1861, this was listed as Clifton Congregational School, and it took in 300 children, a large number of pupils when you consider that there was one schoolmaster and one schoolmistress. It was there that the first company of the Boys' Brigade in Bristol was formed, a movement which was to spread all over the world.

There was virtually no secondary education available in Hotwells and bright pupils had to win scholarships to one of the charity schools, or later, to one of the city-run grammar schools. Difficult boys could also end up at the Clifton Industrial School, once the Clifton poorhouse, and in 1859 turned into a reformatory school, to rescue children at risk of turning to crime. Here boys had an elementary education and were taught manual skills. Instrumental music was a speciality and many boys went on to play in military bands.

They would drill on a terrace below the National School, and the Rev. Frank Downes, in his reminiscences of boyhood in Hotwells, describes the Industrial School as a building which local children were forbidden to go near. He says it closed in 1923, and that soon after it was destroyed by fire. The few remaining foundations have disappeared with redevelopment on the Hotwell Road.

There was also a movement to improve the skills and literacy of adults, and the adult school movement which started in the 1870s reached Hotwells by 1900. These were schools mainly for men (presumably to keep them out of the pubs) and in 1908 Hotwells had an Adult School Club; in the basement men could play punchball, quoits and skittles and upstairs was a reading room, a washhouse and a refreshment bar. There was also a big hall for meetings, talks, entertainments and debates, a billiard room and a games room.

The equivalent resource for women was provided at church and chapel, which provided a vital role in the community, offering spiritual guidance, education, entertainment and practical help: there were cookery classes, sewing bees, and talks on childcare and housewifery. At the Home Encouragement Society Exhibition in Hotwells in 1881, forty houses in Hotwells were entered for the neat and tidy house competition. The cookery judges had to taste forty lots of boiled potatoes and peas.

Hotwells had no shortage of chapels in the nineteenth century. Hope Chapel, built in 1787, catered for the Congregationists, the Methodists went to Grenville Chapel, the Baptists to Buckingham Chapel, and the Brethren to Cumberland Hall.

For the Anglicans there was Trinity Church and Dowry Chapel, an offshoot of St. Andrews up in Clifton, or St. Peter's, at the foot of Jacob's Wells. In addition, there were seven mission halls, run by various denominations.

Religion was central to most people's lives, part of its fabric, in a more religious age, but part of the attraction was the social life the churches, chapels and missions provided, especially for women; The Women's Bright Hour was a weekly highlight.

"Hope Chapel was my father's life, he was a deacon and a teacher, and we attended three times on Sunday and went there most nights of the week for socials, meetings, choir practice and three day sales every year. I was married there and my children were christened there," recalls Molly Sweeney.

Nowadays Hotwells people get their social life, education, entertainment, and food for the spirit from other sources. Except for Hope Chapel and Trinity Church, the buildings that enriched the lives of their grandparents have either been demolished, or in two cases in Hotwells, turned into flats, while another, on the Hotwell Road, is used for a mini-market.

Hope Chapel c.1890.

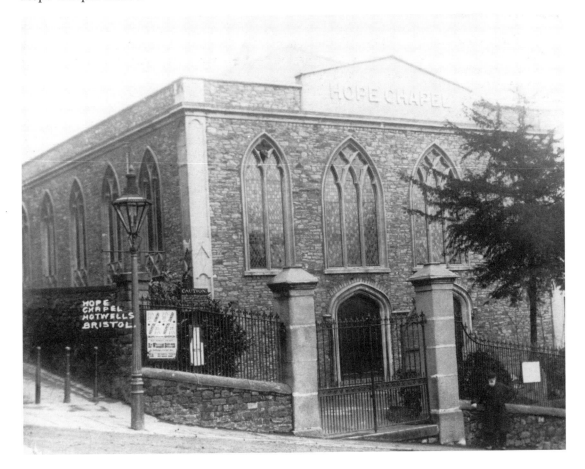

The communal gardens of Dowry Square with a view of St Andrew-the-Less.

A Sunday School outing from St Andrew's in 1953.

St. Andrew=the=Less

DOWRY SQUARE, CLIFTON

Jubilee

1873=1923

Dowry Chapel

Built = = 1744
Closed = = 1872

REV. C. J. SENIOR
1870

REV. E. P. HATHAWAY
1882

REV F. BISHOP
1886

REV S. F. ALFORD
1897

Corner Stone
Laid
Aug. 1872

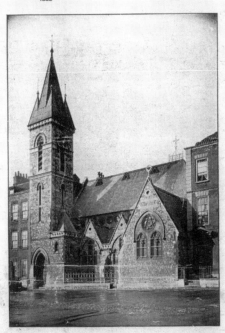

Consecrated
Sept. 24th,
1873

Holy Trinity Church.

Rev. Chadwick, churchwarden Mr Maggs and the choir of Holy Trinity Church.

A meeting of the ladies of Holy Trinity in Cornwallis Gardens. The vicarage there was sold in 1954 to be replaced by the current vicarage at 6 Goldney Avenue.

Members of the community who worked to convert Hope Chapel to Hope Centre in 1977. For over 20 years the building provided a focal point for community events and an exciting arts programme. In 2001 the lease was taken over by Hope Community Church.

The Baptist Chapel on the Hotwell Road, designed by Sir George Oatley, being demolished to make way for student flats.

Hope Chapel was founded by Lady
Henrietta Hope, shocked by the 'goings-on'
at the spa in the eighteenth century. She
died of consumption, the spa waters
failing to help her condition.

The visit of the Marechale drew great crowds to Hope Chapel in March, 1925.

St Peter's Church, Jacob's Wells Road, consecrated in 1882 and closed for worship on March lst, 1938.

Cliftonwood Industrial School, drawn by Samuel Loxton in 1905. Above is Clifton National School, with the terrace where the Industrial School boys did drill railed in below it.

The infants of Hotwells National School.

Hotwell Primary School is an amalgamation of all the other local schools that once existed:
dance group c.1990s.

Hope Square in the 1950s. The houses on the right have been restored, but those on the left were demolished for new flats.

9 Bad Times

When the charitable ladies of Victorian Clifton wanted something to make them feel virtuous, there was no shortage of good works to be done in Hotwells.

Ever since the decline of the spa, as Clifton rose in importance, Hotwells had been in a gentle decline, and by the second half of the nineteenth century there was serious poverty in the slum houses that lined the slopes below Clifton. There were street names which belied their condition: Joy, Love and Hope.

There were periods of prosperity when the docks were busy, but it was not work that could be depended on, and there was no welfare net to catch those who lost their jobs. When times were hard, Hotwells people had to rely on their church or chapel, their friends and charity to keep them going. Anything was better than asking for parish relief, or going to the workhouse.

As we have seen, Hotwells had always been concerned with good or bad health; one of the reasons for the suburb being established at all was the spa water, said to cure everything from dropsy to diabetes, but mainly known (mistakenly) as a cure for TB.

When spas went out of fashion, the Hotwells people had to survive on a private medical system that had to be paid for. With poverty comes bad health, and this was why the Clifton Dispensary was set up in Dowry Square by Thomas Whippie, at his own expense, in 1812.

The dispensary ran on subscription tickets; rich subscribers got four tickets per guinea donation, and these, valid for six weeks, they handed out to the needy sick who asked for one, to get free treatment, or the services of a midwife and the loan of a lying-in outfit. In an emergency, families would have to go from patron to patron, begging for a note. And if they couldn't afford the medicine, they were told to visit Dr. Downs, that is, get some fresh air.

The Dispensary rules said: "The patients of this institution shall be such persons as have no other means of obtaining medical assistance at the time of admission." This medical care was for residents only, and women were only treated if their children had been vaccinated against smallpox. In Dowry Parade there was the grimly named Dispensary For Ulcerated Legs.

When epidemics came, Hotwells always suffered more than healthier, richer Clifton. The cholera epidemic of 1832, reported surgeon John Kerr, "scarcely found its way up the hill, beyond the dirty purlieus of the worst courts in the Hotwell Road, nor has it attacked a single individual above the working class."

The Clifton Dispensary ran as a charity right up to the arrival of the NHS in 1948, and after serving as offices, has now been converted into flats. Another resource for women and children only was the Read Dispensary, opened on St. George's Road in 1874.

Poor health, poverty, and bad housing were interlinked, and all three could be found in abundance in Hotwells, as witnessed by letters to the local paper, the *Clifton Chronicle*. In 1857 a letter mentions "the notoriously poor district of the Hotwells", and in the winter of 1867 there was a report of great destitution:

> Great numbers of poor shivering starving creatures have daily during this inclement weather been relieved by meals of bread and cheese at the Mendicity Office (run by the Clifton charitable). About 200 cases of very great destitution in the Hotwells are at present under investigation.

"I have many a time heaved a heavy sigh over the changing scenes in the Hotwells, compared with 30 years ago," a reader wrote in 1879, "The Hotwell House is boarded up, a receptacle for all sorts of rubbish." In 1884 a correspondent reported on poverty-stricken people on poor relief, fighting the battle of life keenly for a crust of bread. Another letter of 1890 talks of Hotwells being mean and squalid, and says that thankfully, "its decadence in no way affects the reputation or beauty of Clifton."

Part of the problem was that the grand Georgian houses were designed for rich people with servants. When the spa failed, these elegant houses were turned into badly maintained tenements, with large families living in one room, and no sanitation or running water.

There was even worse housing in a network of dark, little alleys and narrow courts off the Hotwell Road on the Clifton Wood side: the names vanished in the slum clearances of the early twentieth century: Avon Square, Norman, Pilliner's, Water's, Jones, Reece's, Allen's and Morgan's Courts, along with Cumberland Cottages have all gone, and the derelict parts of the Hotwell Road, not bombed but simply neglected, are now being replaced with luxury flats.

A graphic description of these dwellings shocked Bristol, when in 1884, the *Times and Mirror* published an investigation,

"The Homes Of The Bristol Poor". There was a slump in shipping and ship-building at the time.

In Hotwells houses, "once the stately homes of the wealthy and great are let out as tenements, and in nobly proportioned rooms where luxury formerly reigned supreme we found last week a family in want of a bit of bread and one woman sleeping on a sack on the bare floor. We found 26 people living in an eight-room house."

In another house, they found "in one room a hobbler, wife and five children, out of work for months, who lived in a room 20 ft square, without any furniture except an old bedstead. The mother and children chopped sticks for firewood, which they sold at 1s. 6d. for two hundredweight. It was not living, it was lingering."

That the tenements in Dowry Square got a better report was due to the work of Susannah Winkworth who was concerned about the welfare of "decent poor people with large families". In the 1860s she took several houses in Dowry Square (ironically now the most expensive properties in Hotwells) which were then "inhabited by a very rough and low set of people," repaired them and in each placed a superintendent to collect the rents and enforce order. The cellars were turned into wash-houses and coal cellars, and the whole character of the square was raised.

She also started a Sanitary Mission, engaging women to go into the homes of the poor and teach them hygiene and house-wifery, and in 1874 she embarked on her plan to build model dwellings for the poor. The result was a block of flats, which exceptionally had gas and water laid on, and balconies, in Jacob's Wells Road. They have since been demolished and replaced by council flats.

The poverty persisted well into the twentieth century; in 1904 a Hotwells teacher reported that 224 children that year required food before going to school. Malnutrition and rickets were common in Hotwells right up to World War Two and the Church Army had to open a hostel for the homeless in Dowry Square during the Depression.

Lebeck House, demolished in 1964 to build Carrick House flats, was in 1740 "an elegantly furnished Tavern", but by early Victorian times an appalling tenement, home to dozens of families. Albert McGrath lived there in the 1920s and recalled that everyone wore jumble clothes, trousers made from sugar bags, and mothers always hoped to get given the Lord Mayor's free heavy boots for their children. There were fleas, bugs, cockroaches, and the fever van came when there were outbreaks of diphtheria and scarlet fever.

The worst of the Hotwell Road slums were cleared in the Twenties and Thirties, with Love Street disappearing to give place to the Hillsborough flats, a model of their kind when they

Sarah Haberfield, 1798–1874, whose charitable bequest enabled Haberfield almshouses to be built on Hotwell Road on the site of the former Royal Gloucester Hotel.

were opened by the Prince of Wales in 1935. Other former slum dwellers were moved to new council housing in other areas of the city.

The Rev. Frank Downes remembered his childish hate of the humiliating weekly visits to the pawnbroker opposite Trinity Church, with bundles of clothes. "But I now realise the pawnbroker was a social necessity, performing a useful and helpful contribution to the needy."

Even more humiliating and distressing was the means test, still bitterly remembered by the elderly. It was carried out when in desperation a family applied for Poor Relief and, as one resident of Haberfield Almshouses remembered, the Guardian would inspect your home rigorously.

"If you had a pair of pictures on the wall they'd say sell them, you couldn't own a rug, or a pack of cards, or a piano but they'd tell you to sell that first before you could have the tokens for food. If one person in the family was in work, they were expected to support the rest, no matter how many of them there were."

The Hotwells shops gave tick, neighbours helped out, the chapels supplied second-hand clothes and toys, and charities soup, but it was the arrival of the Welfare State that transformed lives in Hotwells after their long struggle against poverty.

These flats on Jacob's Wells Road were built for the 'decent poor' by Susannah Winkworth in 1874. They were demolished c.1950 to make way for new city council flats.

Hillsborough flats under construction in 1935. Decrepit buildings in Love Street were pulled down and allotments and an orchard bordering Clifton Vale built on.

Architectural loss: number 274 Hotwell Road – Lebeck House – was demolished in 1960, along with fine adjoining houses and the Church of St Andrew-the-Less, for the Carrick House flats.

Granby Hill
dereliction, c.1950s,
with Mrs Conybear,
well known for her
toffee apples.

Workmen on the
roof of the
'triangular shop' at
the top of Granby
Hill, c.1950s.

The Apothecary's
House on Granby
Hill, 1960s.

Freeland Place houses could easily have been demolished, but for a strenuous campaign by people who 'took a chance' on buying and renovating them.

National Registration No _OAA1. 519/1._ No.122

No 3

NOT TRANSFERABLE

British Overseas Airways Corporation

This ticket is issued to _EDWARD T. WADE_

of _101 PRINCESS VICTORIA STREET_

and admits the person named to the Rocks Railway Shelter subject to the conditions printed on the back hereof.

Issued by ....

The BBC used the Rocks Railway in the early years of the war. They tried out the acoustics when Sir Adrian Boult brought the BBC Symphony Orchestra to Bristol, but were thwarted by desperate locals who staged a sit-in.

10   Hotwells Destroyed

Considering its proximity to the docks, Hotwells got off relatively lightly during the Blitz. It is popularly believed that the decayed sections of the Hotwell Road were the result of bombing, but the main cause was a neglect that has only just ended with the much needed redevelopment of the Mardyke end of this important approach into the city.

There were many small bombs and incendiaries which caused damage in the Hotwell Road, Dowry Parade, Chapel Row and Joy Hill, and the Good Friday raid destroyed Heber Denty's timber sheds, but the major devastation was caused by the worst raid of all, on January 3, 1941, when buildings all along the Hotwell Road were hit.

The cinema, Axten's, and Clifton National School were all damaged so badly that they never re-opened, but the worst damage was inflicted on Trinity Church. The 1829 building, by C.R. Cockerell, was totally gutted and much of it had to be completely rebuilt. The work was completed in 1958 and the interior is now very different from the original design.

But Hotwells did become famous for its unique air raid shelter during the blitzes, the one in the disused railway tunnel on the Portway. Conditions there were so scandalous, and the public desire to be "buried in rock" so strong, that the row over the Portway Tunnel went right to Cabinet level, and many people wrote letters to the King and Queen about it.

That it was a safe place to shelter was borne out by the fact that the Corporation decided to store the city treasures and archives in the driest part of the tunnel. If it was that safe, why weren't people more important than historic objects? Also the BBC secretly planned to have its regional headquarters there should Britain be invaded. So the worst part of the tunnel, a dripping, insanitary dark 525 feet, was taken over in November 1940 by local people, who devised a kind of indoor camp, with portable toilets, sacking curtains and make-shift beds.

"Your couldn't lie out, you stood up or knelt, cooped up with your back against the wall, and it was streaming with water . . . because there were no doors in the tunnel you couldn't close it off and people would arrive in the night, especially when a raid was taking place. It was sheer panic."

The authorities tried to stop them, but word spread and as many as 3,000 people came from all over the city to queue after work to try for a place in this hell-hole: they even fought to get in. When an insensitive attempt was made to evict the residents and close the shelter down, there was a sit-in and though the police were called, they decided not to intervene.

Eventually the civil authorities had to back down, and they cleaned the tunnel out, made it minimally waterproof, installed bunks, and limited occupation for 200. A few more people were allowed to sit on the steps inside the Rocks Railway, which by then had closed, but the way the shelterers were treated rankled for years.

Those who sheltered there as children recall the darkness and the stink but also a strong social life, when posh people from Clifton made friends with the working class Hotwellians. Some still believe the Portway tunnel saved their lives.

There were other shelters, in the gardens and squares – in hot weather the outline of the one in Hope Square is still visible – and the rest of the city thought Hotwells folk were fortunate to live in eighteenth-century houses because they had deep cellars to shelter in.

After the war, Hotwells continued to decay. Though the Merchant's Road side had been much improved by the arrival of the late-Victorian and Edwardian villas of Sandford and Oldfield Road, the Georgian parts of the suburb gently collapsed. It was not bombing that destroyed the Granby Hill section of Hope Square, but neglect and absentee landlords. The big old houses were multi-occupied, some of them by homeless squatters and tramps, though it must be said that much of Clifton was equally seedy and decayed.

Post-war planners in Bristol took the view that they were doing the citizens a favour by pulling down these old insanitary terraces and replacing them with modern flats with modern amenities. It was fortunate that they did not turn their attention to Hotwells until the late 60s, when the tide for conservation was on the turn.

The middle-class poor who admired Georgian architecture but couldn't afford Clifton moved down the hill, led by Peter Ware, who rescued the beautiful north-east corner house in Dowry Square, and set an example that others followed. Gradually, the big houses were restored, often in the nick of time. The remaining wing of Hope Square was saved from demolition at the last minute, when the council decided to let a group of local people restore the entire row of houses.

Now, of course, Hotwells is a desirable area to live in, and the despised eighteenth-century houses are much sought-after, but people forget what a near thing it was, and how many Hotwells houses were only saved because they were finally listed as being of historic interest, thus making demolition harder.

The other big changes were caused by attending to traffic needs. First, came the Portway, which brought in new traffic from the north of the city, and then in April 1965, the Cumberland Basin flyover opened. Three and a half hours after the Transport Minister cut the tape, the Plimsoll Bridge jammed open and there was traffic chaos, something Hotwells has suffered ever since, when the bridges swing, or there is an accident.

The scheme was needed because traffic from the Somerset side was having to cross the New Cut on the old double-decker road-and-rail bridge, and the river at the narrow bridge by the Nova Scotia. When these bridges were swung, the bottleneck, described as the worst in the West, was intolerable, and with car ownership growing, and motorways being built, something had to be done, even if the docks closure loomed and only pleasure craft and sandboats would need to get through the dock.

The Hotwells that was lost to the flyover was a long triangle on the river bank, an area from the bottom of Granby Hill to Merchant's Road. Three entire streets, Caroline, Brunswick and Grenville Place, were demolished and their inhabitants rehoused; several shops and five pubs went, the Rownham Hotel, the General Draper, the Pilot, the Star and the Swansea Arms; the old eighteenth-century Long Room was flattened, along with Cumberland Hall, the end of Freeland Place was chopped off, and the 150-year-old Dockmaster's House was blown up, clock tower and all. People moved away.

The project cost £2,650,000, took five years from planning to opening, 35 homes were acquired for demolition at a cost of £230,000, several shop-keepers went out of business, the volume of traffic multiplied, choking Hotwells with ever more fumes, and the residents lost their ancient views of the water.

With touching naivety, the planners sought to compensate Hotwellians who they said had co-operated almost 100 per cent with the scheme, by giving them a "piazza" under the flyover. Under and amid the traffic, "the centre of life will be a piazza with a pool and fountain with water displays of changing form and colours, green spaces, children's playgrounds, open air cafés and seats to watch the ships go by." Ho hum.

The entrance to the Portway Tunnel air-raid shelter. When the first air raids started on November 24th, 1940, over 3,000 people fought for places inside.

Firemen at work in the burnt-out interior of Holy Trinity church following the devastating air-raid of January 3rd, 1941.

Ambra Vale victory party, with street decorations strung between concrete and brick air-raid shelters.

Coronation party in Brunswick Place and Caroline Place in 1953. Most of these homes would be demolished in the 1960s, only the Rose of Denmark and adjoining houses surviving.

Hotwells shortly before the 1960s destruction. Brunswick Place and Caroline Place were major casualties, but on the south of the basin, Cabbage Garden allotments and the cattle pens (receiving animals from Ireland) would also make way for the flyover complex.

Much of this corner of Hotwells, including Sopey Park, disappeared under the new concrete.

Buildings to disappear from the Hotwells scene included, in the foreground, Dumbleton's Garage, the Territ Memorial Hall and the public lavatories.

The Dock Master's House, an imposing Italianate building demolished in the 1960s mayhem. The clock survives at the city's Industrial Museum.

The centre of Hotwells before it was altered to improve the road system.

Cumberland Basin 1960s reconstruction in progress.

After the bulldozers had gone. Brunswick Place and Caroline Place once stood on the cleared land.

Rescued and restored: s.s.*Great Britain*, part of the continuing Hotwells story.

11 Hotwells Reborn

Apart from being briefly fashionable as a spa, Hotwells was always considered to be a working class suburb, whose residents worked in the docks, ran shops or worked as servants in Clifton.

This image of Hotwells persisted well into the 1980s, for even then the district was still rated by the council as a deprived area. Though the elegant houses were being restored, and the tightly knit community was thriving, the fact that the docks had closed, leaving sad industrial remains behind, that so many shops had gone, and that there was little work in the area, combined to create a negative view of the area.

All it needed was a change of mind-set. Once the council and the developers began to see the former docks as an asset, a leisure area where waterside homes would be eagerly sought after, attitudes changed completely and, once again, Hotwells is chic.

The commercial river traffic has gone but instead there are the yachts and canoes; the former sand and coal wharves have become marinas, and the disused dock buildings have been brought back to life as pubs and restaurants, or art galleries. The Underfall is now regarded as an important piece of industrial archaeology, and the old bonded warehouses have found new uses, such as the Create Centre and Bristol Record Office.

It probably started in 1970 with the symbolic return and then restoration of Brunel's *Great Britain*, and the realisation that the old docks could become an important maritime heritage site. Once the dead water became alive again with ferries and pleasure boats, the deserted waterside became interesting to developers.

They kicked off by building Rownham Mead, on the site of the old cattle sheds, and now all along the Hotwell Road, luxury homes are going up in the ugly gaps that had been an eyesore for almost a century. Poole's Wharf recycled some of the old dock offices, and the former timber sheds are sites for upmarket expensive homes. The yards and offices of long-gone businesses are being transformed and the area is booming.

Paradoxically, Hotwells, which once depended so heavily on the docks for employment, owes its renaissance to their closure. As ever, water is what makes Hotwells bubble.

The *Matthew* in the entrance lock.

A view of the marina, with Southernhay on the hillside.

The newly restored Patent Slip at Underfall Yard.

Behind the trees is Spike Island, now home to professional artists, formerly a Brooke Bond tea factory.

A boat from Baltic Wharf Sailing School in front of the bridge across Hotwell Dock linking housing on Poole's Wharf with Rownham Mead.

Victoria Terrace: least changed of all Hotwells streets and terraces.

The modern Hotwells. 'Not brilliant architecture,' says Tony Aldous of the Poole's Wharf housing in *C20: Bristol's Twentieth-Century Buildings*, 'but it has a personality of its own.'